Samsung S5

User Guide

Disclaimer

Report Summary

Have you recently purchased the next big thing, the Samsung Galaxy S5, and have no idea what to do with it or how to operate it? Well you are in luck. This S5 manual will give you a brilliant insight into the phone and will tell you about all the features that this phone has to offer to its users. The phone is truly amazing because of the brand new apps and facilities that were never there in the Galaxy series before.

The step by step guide will ensure that no matter what questions you will have regarding this phone, it will all be available to you through this, and you will not have to look anywhere else.

Contents

Introduction

The launch of the new Samsung Galaxy S5 was officially announced at an event in Barcelona and the phone is a big improvement from its predecessor, the Samsung Galaxy S4. Showcasing a bigger screen, an amazing upgrade in the camera, and a great amount of power, the phone is categorized as a superphone for the year 2014.

The phone also features some of the newest features, one of which particularly focuses on the health of the phone's owner. With this phone, you will likely feel all the more powerful, and in better control of your daily lifestyle.

Getting Started

Device layout

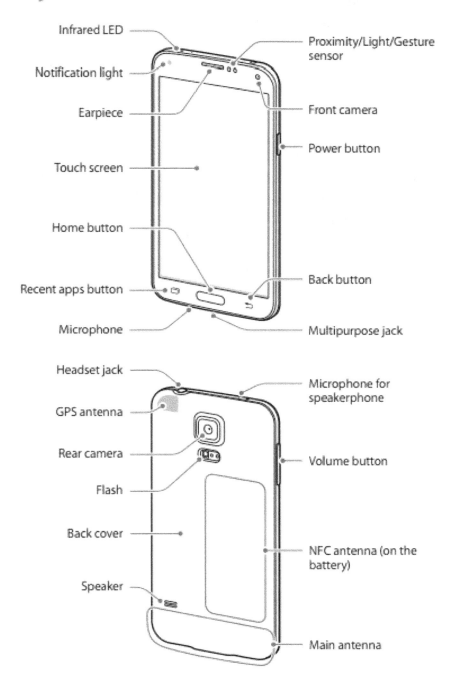

Infrared LED

Notification light

Earpiece

Touch screen

Home button

Recent apps button

Microphone

Proximity/Light/Gesture sensor

Front camera

Power button

Back button

Multipurpose jack

Headset jack

GPS antenna

Rear camera

Flash

Back cover

Speaker

Microphone for speakerphone

Volume button

NFC antenna (on the battery)

Main antenna

Important Phone Buttons

Power

The power button lets you turn your phone on and off by simply pressing and holding onto it. The phone will automatically go into the lock mode once the screen is off.

Recent Apps

You can tap onto this to open up the list of your recent app visits. If you hold onto this option, you will open up additional options.

Home

You can unlock your phone by pressing onto your home button. This button is also used if you want to return to your home screen at any point. When you press this button twice, you will open up S voice. Upon pressing and holding the button, Google will launch.

Back

You can tap onto this to return to your prior screen.

Volume

This is used to adjust the volume of your phone.

Basics

Touchscreen

You can use your finger to tap into whatever you want to use. If you want to use your phone's keyboard or go onto a certain app, all can be done with a simply tap of your finger onto your screen.

You can use the tap and hold option on a particular item to see more option available with respect to that item. If you want to drag an item from one place to another, all you have to do is hold it and then drag it using your finger only.

You can double tap on a certain image or webpage to zoom it in. zoom out can easily be done by double tapping on it again. You can also zoom in and out by spreading two of your fingers apart or pinching in your two fingers respectively.

If you want to visit different panels on your apps or home screen, then all you have to do if use a flicking motion on your screen using your finger.

Quick Setting Panel and Notifications

Notifications Panel

Your status bar will start showing certain indicator icons whenever you receive missed calls or new messages. When you want to view these in detail, you can simply open up your notifications panel and you will be able to do so.

You can open this panel by dragging the bar downwards. To close it, simply flick this bar from bottom to an upwards direction using your finger.

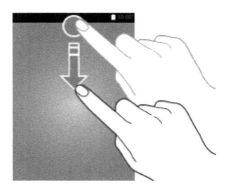

Notifications panel Functions

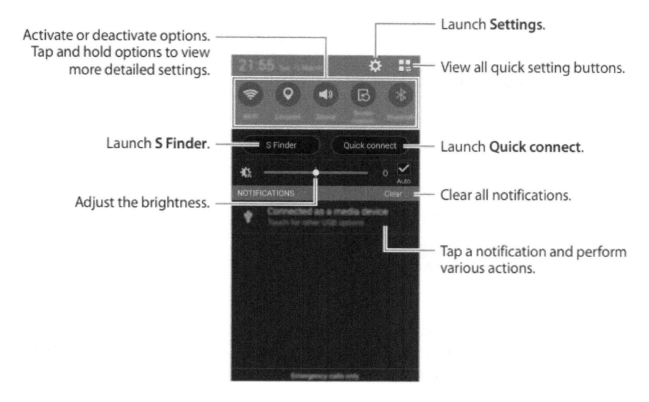

Activate or deactivate options.
Tap and hold options to view
more detailed settings.

Launch **Settings**.

View all quick setting buttons.

Launch **S Finder**.

Launch **Quick connect**.

Adjust the brightness.

Clear all notifications.

Tap a notification and perform
various actions.

Brightness Adjustment

For automatic adjustment of the brightness, you can select "Auto". For manual
adjustment, you can drag the bar yourself either to the right or the left. On low battery,
this bar for brightness adjustment simply disappears from the panel.

Quick Setting Panel

There are a wide number of options available for quick setting in the panel for notifications. You can open up the quick setting panel for even further options. This option will help you to either activate or deactivate certain options and features. You can open up your quick panel by dragging down the status bar using two fingers.

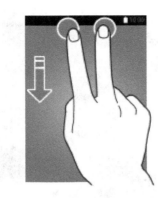

Some of the options included in the quick setting panel are Location, Wi-Fi, Bluetooth, screen rotation, smart pause, screen mirroring, smart stay power saving, private mode, Multi Window, and mobile data.

Apps and Home Screens

Home Screen

You home screen is the first thing that you get to see on your phone. It shows various shortcuts to different apps, widgets, and many more things. There are also various panels situated on the home screen and to view all of them you will have to swipe your finger towards the right or left direction. For home screen customization, you can go onto the "Managing the Home and Apps screens".

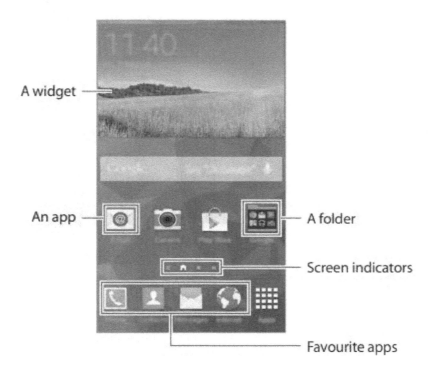

My Magazine on Your Home Screen

There is a My Magazine option on your home screen which lets you view all of the latest news and updates from social media that you would like to see. You can choose the content that you would like to be displayed for you on My Magazine simply by going onto "Settings" and then choose whatever you like.

You can also select "Auto Refresh on Opening" to automatically update any new content on this tool. If you are no longer interested in "My Magazine, you can deactivate the tool by holding a certain area of your home screen with your finger then tapping into "Home Screen Settings". From here you can deactivate "My Magazine".

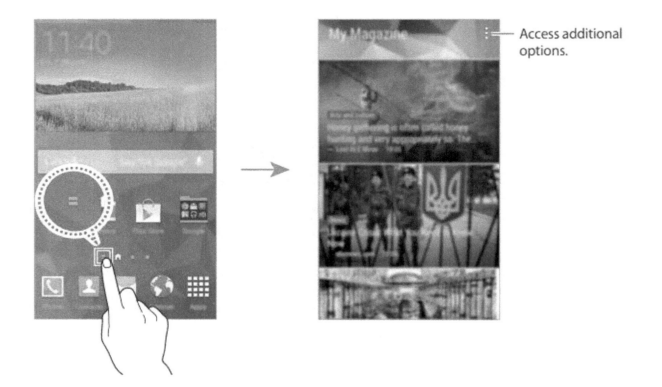

Access additional options.

Apps Screen

Your Apps screen will show all of your apps related icons, even the apps that you might have recently installed into your phone. You can tap onto the "Apps" icon from your Home Screen to access your Apps Screen. While there, you can see all your apps by scrolling right or left. A screen indicator is also situated at the screen bottom which you can use to go to another panel. You have the option of customizing your Apps screen by visiting the "Managing the Home and Apps Screens" option.

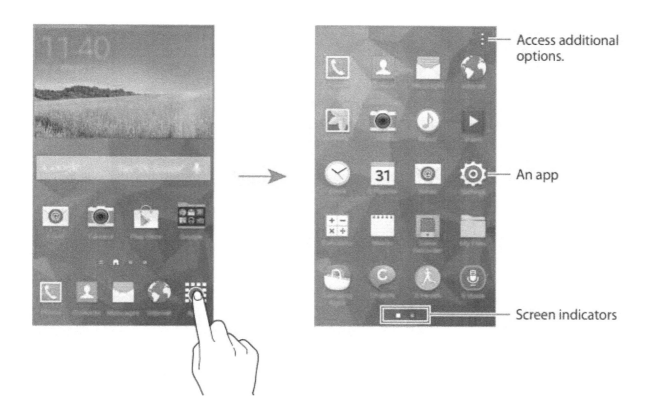

Access additional options.

An app

Screen indicators

Power Saving Feature

Power Saving Mode

You can save the battery power of your phone by limiting some of its functions. To activate this, go onto your Apps Screen and tap onto "Settings". From there, go on "Power Saving" and then "Power Saving Mode". You can also go on quick setting panel and tapping onto the "Power Saving" option.

This will then give you a list of options to choose from, such as, Restrict Performance, Block Background Data, and Greyscale Mode.

Ultra Power Saving Mode

You have this option to further extend the battery life of your phone. In this mode, you phone will display gray tone colors, limit access to some of the apps, deactivate mobile data on off screen, and deactivate Bluetooth and Wi-Fi.

You can activate this by going onto your apps screen and then selecting "Settings" from there. Then, you should tap on "Power Saving" and then from there "Ultra Power Saving".

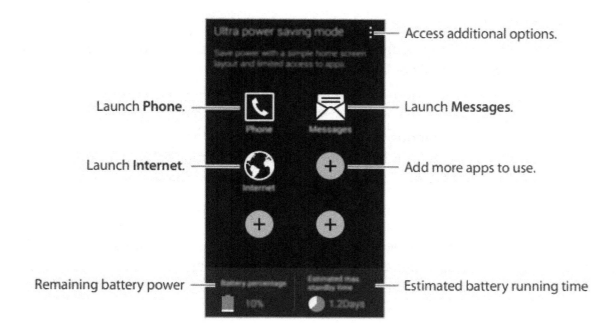

Access additional options.

Launch **Phone**.

Launch **Messages**.

Launch **Internet**.

Add more apps to use.

Remaining battery power

Estimated battery running time

Installing and Uninstalling Your Apps

Samsung Apps

You can use your Samsung apps to buy and then download these apps. Access them by tapping onto "Samsung Apps" from your Apps screen.

Installation of Apps

You can browse through various apps by either searching for them or searching by categories. Once you have found your preferred app, you can tap on it for viewing further details. Free apps are available under the caption of "Free".

Play Store

This is an app especially designed to get access to other games and various apps that can function on your phone without hassle. To access this app, all you have to do is go on "Play Store" available on your Apps Screen.

Installation of Apps

You can either search for your respective app or browse various apps within a certain category. If you wish to install a certain app, you can tap on it to know more information with regards to that app.

Suggested Apps Download

You can look for as well as download certain apps that are specific to your Galaxy phone. In order to do this, all you have to do is go on your Apps screen. From then access more options and then tap onto "Galaxy Essentials". You can even access this directly from your Home Screen and then download it. if you wish to download all of the suggested apps, then you can do so by tapping on "Download All".

Apps Management

Un-installation of Apps

You can uninstall apps that you do not require anymore, but downloaded previously, by simply going onto your Apps screen and then tapping on more options. In the more options, you will be able to find "Downloaded Apps" in which you will find further options. On that, you can simply tap on "Uninstall". You can also go on settings from your Apps Screen and then to "application Manager". From here you will be able to choose any app you do not want anymore, and then tap on "Uninstall".

If you want to uninstall or disable a default app, then you will have to go onto your Apps screen. From there tap onto the sign of further options. Then go to "Uninstall/Disable apps and then disable your respective app.

Enable Apps

To enable certain apps, you will have to go to your Apps Screen, and then from there go onto further option. In further options, you will be able to find "Show Disabled Apps". Tap on this option, select a particular app, and then tap on "Done". You can also carry out this process by going onto your Apps Screen, then tapping on "Settings", and then from there going onto "Application Manager". In the application manager, you will find the option of "Disabled". Tap on that, then choose your respective app, and then tap on "Enable".

Personalizing

Easy Mode

The easy mode on your phone provides you with the opportunity to have a much easier and simpler user experience with your phone with cons that are bigger and a layout that is simpler. Easy mode also lets you access some of your settings that have been frequently used and all your popular apps, along with adding shortcuts to your contacts that are in the favorite category.

You can access easy mode by going onto your Apps screen. From there you can tap into settings. Within settings, you will find the option of "Easy Mode". After that, you can simply choose the apps that you want a simpler layout of and then select "Done".

If you want to come back to standard mode, you can go onto your Home Screen, and then go on Easy Settings. After that, you can choose Easy Mode, and then "Standard Mode", and then finally tap on "Done".

Managing App and Home Screens

Managing Home Screen

Addition of Items

To add items onto the home screen, all you need to do is simply tap and hold onto a certain folder or app from your Apps Screen, and then drag this onto the Home Screen. You can also add widgets onto the Home screen by tapping and holding onto an empty area and then from the options selecting "Widgets". Next, tap and hold onto a certain widget and then drag it onto your home screen.

Removing or Moving an Item

To move an item from your home screen, you are required to tap and hold onto the item, and then drag it along to the new location. For moving an item towards another panel, simply drag the item towards the screen side. Also, you can use the shortcuts area which is located at your home screen bottom to move all your apps that you frequently make use of.

Finally, you can remove a certain item from your home screen by tapping and then holding onto it, and then dragging it to the "Remove" option that will mist definitely appear at your screen top.

Folder Creation

You can create a folder by going onto the Home screen and then from there tapping and holding onto a certain app. Ten you can drag this app to a "Create Folder" option that will appear on top of your screen.

After this is done, you can enter your respective folder name and then choose the apps that you want to move to that respective folder. After you are done with all this, you can click on "Done".

Panel management

On your Home Screen, tap and hold onto an empty where you can remove, add, or move a panel. In order to add a certain panel, you can scroll towards the left to your last panel and then tap onto the + sign. In order to move a certain panel, you can tap and hold onto a panel preview, and then drag this towards a new point. In order for you to remove a certain panel, tap and hold onto your panel review, and then drag this to the "Remove" option towards the top of your screen. You can even set a certain panel as your main Home Screen by tapping onto the icon that looks like a house.

Managing Your Apps Screen

Change View Mode

You can change your view mode by going onto your Apps screen and then tapping onto more options. Within more options, you will then be required to tap onto "View As" and then selecting your relevant method of sorting.

Hide Apps

You can hide your apps that you do not want seen anymore on you Apps Screen. To do this, you will be required to go onto your apps screen and then tap into more options. In more options, you will find the option of "Hide Apps. Click that and then tap onto select apps, after which you are required to tap onto "Done".

Move Items

In order to move items, you will have to go onto your Apps screen. From there, you will be required to tap onto more options and select "Edit". After this, tap and hold onto a certain item and drag it towards a new position. You can move a certain item to a different panel by dragging it towards the side of your screen. In order for you to move a certain item to a different panel, you can drag it to the "Create Page" option and this option appears at your screen top.

Create Folders

You can create a folder by going onto your Apps screen and then tapping onto more options. From more options, you will select the option of "Create Folder". You can also tap onto more options and then select "Edit", and then from there tapping and holding onto a certain app and then dragging it onto your "Create Folder" option. This option will be appearing on your screen top.

After this you will be required to give your folder a certain relevant name, and then choose all the apps that you would like to be in this folder. Once you are finally done, you can select "Done".

Changing Your Screen Lock

You can put up a desired screen lock so that unauthorized users do not access your personal information. Set this up by going onto your Apps Screen and then from there tapping onto settings. In settings, you will find the option of "Lock Screen" and in that you will find "Screen Lock". There are various types of screen locks:

Pattern

This is where you connect four or maybe more dots together to form some pattern. You can also set up a PIN backup in the case where you forget your pattern.

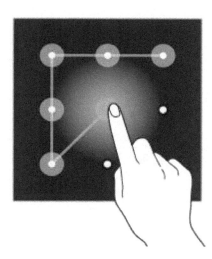

Fingerprints

You can use your Finger Scanner to officially unlock your phone using your fingerprints.

PIN

A PIN will only have number. You can enter your desired PIN and use it as your password.

Password

A password will feature both numbers and characters.

Wallpaper Setup

You can set up a wallpaper for your phone by going onto your Apps screen and then going on "Settings". From there you can go onto "Wallpaper. You can also do this by holding onto an empty area within your home screen and then tapping onto "Wallpaper".

You can then search on your device for a perfect image or photo to be put up as your wallpaper.

Ringtone Change

You have the option of changing your ringtone for your notifications and incoming call. All you have to do is go onto your Apps Screen, and then from there tap onto settings and then "Sound". For incoming calls, you will have to then tap onto "Ringtones", then select a suitable ringtone and then tap on OK. For your notifications, you will have to tap onto notifications, then select a suitable ringtone, and then tap on OK.

Connecting to a Network

Mobile Network

When your Wi-Fi connection or any Wi-Fi network is not available to you, then you have the option of connecting your phone with a mobile network. For this, you can go onto your Apps screen, and then from there tap onto "Settings". In your settings, you will have the option of "Data Usage". Tick on "Mobile Data" in that option. You can also do this by going onto your quick setting panel and then tapping onto "Mobile Data".

Wi-Fi Network

You can connect your mobile to any Wi-Fi network that is available to you, and then log onto the internet with it. You can also go onto your Wi-Fi option to check out the additional options that are available to you. If you wish to conserve your battery, you can turn your Wi-Fi off.

You can access your Wi-Fi by going onto your Apps screen and then "Settings" from there. You can also access this from your quick setting panel. After this, you can choose your appropriate network from a list of given networks and then tap onto connect.

Usability and Motions

Control Motions

Air Browse

You can Air Browse by going on to your Apps Screen, then going onto "Settings", then "Motions and Gestures", and then finally "Air Browse". You can then activate this option.

After air browse has been activated, you can move up or down, and left or right by moving you hand in the respective motion over the sensor.

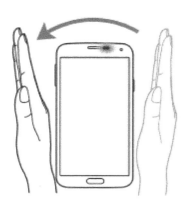 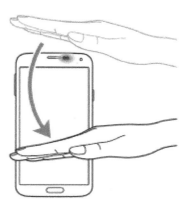

Direct Call

You can set up Direct Call by going onto settings from your Apps screen, and then tapping on "Motions and Gestures". From there you can go on the "Direct Call" option and activate it.

After this option has been activated, you can place your phone directly to your ear while you view a particular contact's message, call, or contact details. This will let you make a call directly.

Smart Alert

For Smart Alert, you will have to go to your Apps screen. From there, click on "Settings", then "Motions and Gestures", and then finally "Smart Alert". Smart alert gives you a heads by if you have had any new messages or missed calls by vibrating once you pick the phone up after it has not been in use for some time.

Pause or Mute

For this, go onto your Apps screen, and then from there tap into "Settings". In your settings option, you will find "Motions and Gestures". Go on that, and then tap into Mute/Pause and activate it.

Once this option is activated, you can silence any alarms or incoming messages by putting your palm on top of your screen. You can also pause any songs that are playing or any active media with the same method.

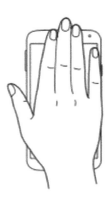

You also have the option, then, to turn your device over to pause any media or mute any alarms and incoming calls.

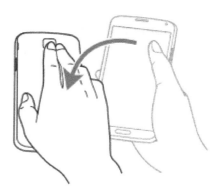

There is also the option of Smart Pause where your device will automatically pause any playback media once you look away from it. If you start looking t it again it will start playing.

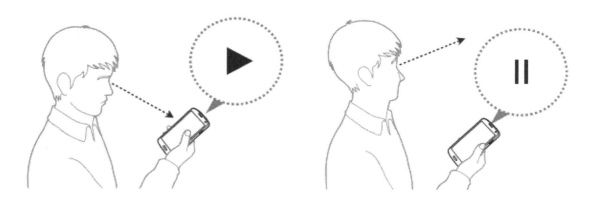

Capture Screen

Go onto your Apps screen and then tap onto "Settings". From there you can go onto "Motions and Gestures" and click on "Capture Screen". Activate this option and you will be able to screenshot anything by putting your hand's side onto the screen and in a sweeping motion going from left to right or right to left. You screenshot will then be saved in your gallery in a specific screenshots folder.

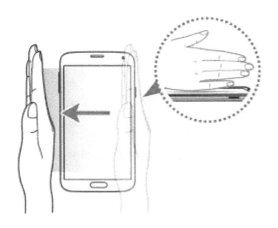

Air View

This feature can be used to do tasks while hovering your finger on the screen. With this mode active, you can even point to see certain content or information. You can activate this by going on your App Screen. From there go onto "Settings" and then "Air View" and activate this option.

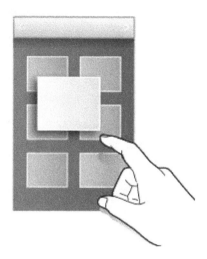

Multi Window

The multi window option on this phone lets you use two of the apps together on a single screen. This means that you can check your emails and see a video all at the same time.

Multi Widow Launch

You can activate the multi window option by going onto your App screen. From there, go onto "Settings", and then tap the "Multi Window" option. You can also activate this option by opening up quick setting panel and then tapping into "Multi Window".

Toolbox

Your toolbox lets you launch a lot of apps while you are still on other apps. You can activate your Toolbox option by going onto quick setting panel and then from there tapping onto "Toolbox". You can also go to Toolbox by going onto your Apps screen, and then from there tapping into "Settings", and then finally "Toolbox".

One Handed Operation

The one handed operation options allows you to operate your phone with just a single hand. You can activate this option by going onto Apps screen, and then from there tapping into "Settings". In the settings option, you will find the "one Handed Operation" option. You can then activate this option.

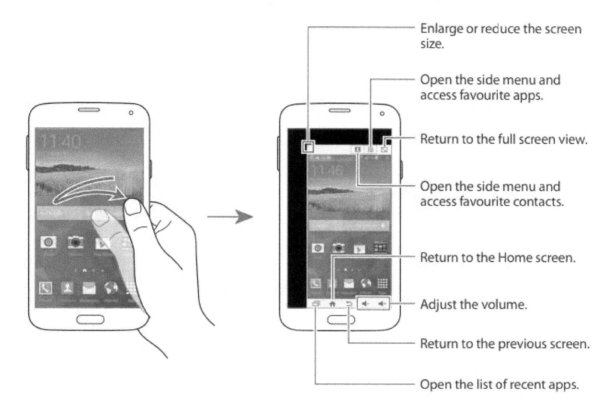

Enlarge or reduce the screen size.

Open the side menu and access favourite apps.

Return to the full screen view.

Open the side menu and access favourite contacts.

Return to the Home screen.

Adjust the volume.

Return to the previous screen.

Open the list of recent apps.

Increasing Sensitivity of Touch Screen

This feature lets you use your phone even if you have gloves put on. You can increase your phone's sensitivity by going onto your Apps screen. From there, tap onto "Settings" and then go on "Display". Over there, you can tick on the option of "Increase Touch Sensitivity". You can also activate this option by going onto quick setting panel, and then from there tapping onto "Increase Touch Sensitivity".

Phone

Calls

When you want to make calls or view your contacts, then you can simply tap the phone option in your Apps. In this, you will have multiple of options. A Keypad will let you type in a phone number, and then by pressing on the "Dial" button you can make a call. For video calling, you can press the "Video Call" situated on the left of the "Dial" button.

You also have the option of making a call by visiting 'Favorites", "Logs", and "Contacts".

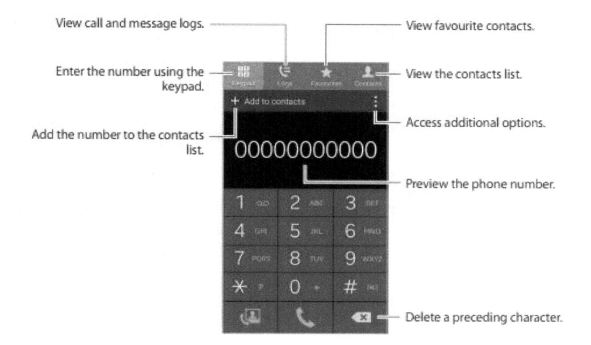

Calls from Contact Lists and Call Logs

To make calls using these, you simply have to tap into one of the options, then using your fingers, drag a phone number or a contact towards the right and your call can be made. You can deactivate this feature by going on settings, then contacts, and then simply unselect the option of "Swipe to call or send msg".

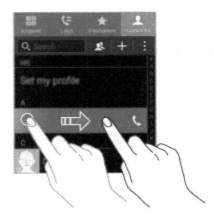

Calls from Favorites List

The contacts that you are in touch with often through calls can easily be transferred into your favorites section. You can do this by tapping on "Contacts", selecting a particular contact, and then pressing on the star sign. Once you have contacts in your "Favorites" category, you can simply go on it, select a particular contact, and then make a call.

Speed Dialing

For speed dialing, tap on the "Keypad" option. Then, hold the number you want associated with a particular contact and tap on "OK". Select the contact you want on this speed dial number and you are done. Another method is to directly go on contacts and then in other options click on the speed dial option.

International Calls

For making an international call, you need to go on your "Keypad". Them, hold the 0 digit and you will that a + sign will appear. You will then be required to enter in the country and area code, along with the desired phone number. After this, simply press the call option.

You can also block all the international outgoing calls by going on settings, then call, then more settings, and then finally call barring. From there you can unselect the "International Calls" option.

Call Receiving

Answering

When you receive a call, simply drag the call option outside of the bigger circle. When using an app however during the time that you receive a call, all you have to do is tap on the "Answer" option in the pop up window.

With call waiting, you can make another call, and while you are on the other call, the first one will be put on hold.

Rejecting

When you receive a call, which you do not want to pick up, then all you have to do is drag the 'reject option outside of the bigger circle. If a call comes while you are involved in using an app, then simply tap on "Reject" in the pop up window. You can even send a message to the rejected call by dragging upwards the reject message bar.

Automatic Unwanted Number Rejection

For this, you can tap the "Phone" option in your Apps. After this, go on settings, then call, then call rejection, then auto reject mode, and then auto reject numbers. You can create an auto reject list where you can assign numbers and categories, and then click on save.

Missed Calls

When you miss a call, the missed call sign will appear in your status bar. You can view this easily by opening your notifications. You can also view your missed calls by going on your apps, and tapping on "Phone" and then from there going on "Logs" to see all your missed calls.

Contacts

Adding Your Contacts

Manually Creating Contacts

In your Apps go on Contacts and in that option you will see a '+' sign. Tap on that and then enter your desired contact information. You can even add in an image of your contact. Click on "Save" after you are done. You can even add in your contact directly from your keypad by going on your keypad, entering your desired number, and then tapping on "Add to Contacts".

Creating Contacts through Business Cards

You can do this by taking a picture of the business card, and then extracting the information in it. Go on your Apps and then tap on "Contacts". After this, go on the "Business cards" option and click on the "+" sign. You can go to the "Target Language" option if you have another language you want recognized. After you are done with that, put the business card on a desk, and take a picture in a landscape orientation. The picture will automatically be taken once the card is properly inside the screen frame.

You always have the option of adding more information or editing the business card contact details before finally tapping on "Save".

Managing Your Contacts

Editing

Tap on "Contacts" in your Apps Screen and after deciding on a contact you want edited, click on the edit option which will be marked with a pencil sign. After you have edited your contact information you can tap on "Save".

Deleting and Sharing

To delete a particular contact simply go on 'more options and press "Delete". If you want to share a contact, all you have to do is select a particular contact and in more options select "Share name card" followed by the method you wish to share with.

Searching

To search for your contacts, go onto your Apps screen and click on "Contacts". In the contacts option, you can either scroll through the contact list to search for your contact, search your contact through the search field on top, or drag your finger through the index towards the right to scroll through the list quickly.

Email and Messages

Messages

Send Messages

With messages, you can either send in multimedia messages or text messages. In order to perform this task, you have to tap on the "Messages" option in your Apps screen, and then tap on the write message option. This is where you can type in your message and add the recipients you want to send the message to. After this, you can click on the send message option.

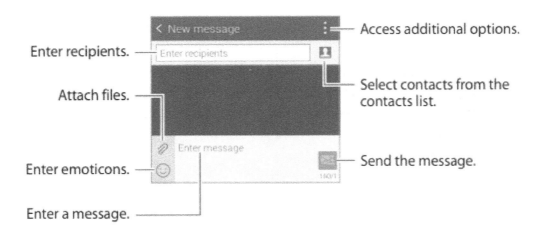

Enter recipients.

Attach files.

Enter emoticons.

Enter a message.

Access additional options.

Select contacts from the contacts list.

Send the message.

View Incoming Messages

All your incoming messages will be grouped together in a thread form according to your sender. You can choose a particular contact in your folder to view all their previous messages.

Email

Set up Email Accounts

Go on your Apps screen and then tap the "Email" option. You can then set your email account up by entering your email address along with your password. After then, you have to click on "Next" if you are in the process of setting up a private account. For a company account, you will have to click on "Manual setup". You can continue with the instructions after that. For another email account, all you have to do is go on "Manage Accounts" and click on the "+" sign.

Send Messages

Tap on your "Email" option in your Apps screen. From there you can type in your subject, recipient's addresses, and the respective message, after which you can hit send. You can attach respective videos and images, along with inserting special events and images. You also have the option of taking recipient information from your contacts list.

Read Messages

On your Apps screen, go to the "Email" option. From there, select the email account you would like to use. When you open that, you will be able to view all your new messages. After this, you can tap on any message you would like to read.

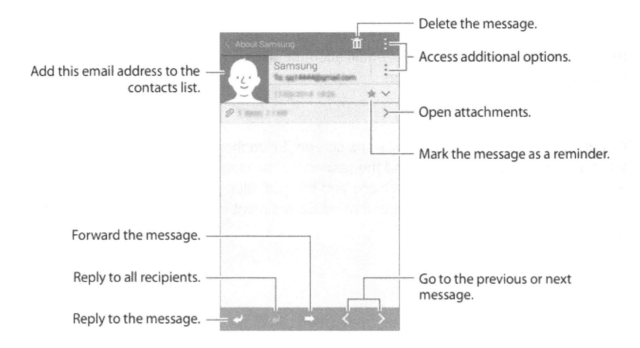

Add this email address to the contacts list.

Delete the message.

Access additional options.

Open attachments.

Mark the message as a reminder.

Forward the message.

Reply to all recipients.

Reply to the message.

Go to the previous or next message.

Google Mail

Delete the message. ─────────────

Keep the message for long-term storage. ─────────────

Mark the message as unread. ─────────

Access additional options. ─────────

Mark the message as a reminder. ─────────

Reply to the message. ─────────

Preview attachment. ─────────

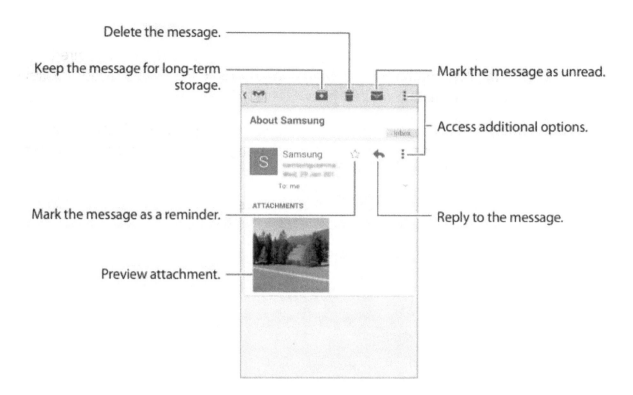

Camera

Taking Pictures and Making Videos

You can use the video and photo app to either take pictures or make your desired videos. After you have taken photos and made videos, you can go on "Gallery" to view all of these any time you want.

To use your camera, you can go on your Apps screen and tap on the "Camera" option. In the preview screen, you can tap on the image to bring the camera into focus. When focus is set, the frame will turn to green.

After this, you can either make a video or take a picture.

Switch between the front and rear camera.

Display current mode.

Start taking a video.

Activate or deactivate selective focus mode.

Take a photo.

Activate or deactivate HDR (Rich tone).

Change the shooting mode.

Change camera settings.

View photos and videos you have taken.

Launching the Camera from Your Locked Screen

When you have to turn your camera on quickly for capturing a special moment that is not going to last long, you can launch you camera from the locked screen by dragging the camera option on your screen outside of the big circle. This will launch the camera, after which you can bring your screen to focus and then take a snap quickly or even make a video.

Dual Camera

You can take a self portrait and a landscape picture together using this dual camera option. When a landscape picture is taken using the rear camera, the movement captured with the front camera shows in the inset window and vice versa. For this option, you will have to go to "Camera, then click on "Mode", and then the "Dual Camera" option.

Switch between the front and rear camera.

Tap to resize it or move the location.

Select among various styles that are available.

Filters

You can use the option of 'filter effects' to make your pictures and videos unique and distinctive. To use this option, you will have to go on "Camera" from your Apps screen, and then go on Effects. From there, you can select a particular effect you want. You can even download a lot more effects by tapping on the "Download" option. You can hide certain effects or change the effects order by going onto "Manage effects".

Zoom Feature

You can zoom into and out of the screen while you make videos or take pictures. For doing this, you can either you can either use two of your fingers to zoom in and out, or you can use the zoom in and zoom out option which is available in your phone.

Virtual Tour Mode

This shooting mode lets you take pictures by rotating right, left, or moving forward. You can take photos with different angles and then later on view them as a slideshow. You can go about this by going onto your "Camera" option, and then tapping onto "Mode". From here, you will be required to tap on "Virtual Tour Shot".

Gallery

Viewing of the Content

You can view the content by tapping onto the "Gallery" option from your Apps screen. After this, you can choose a particular image or even multiple images by tapping on them. In case of multiple images, you will have to hold the image one by one until a 'tick' sign appears.

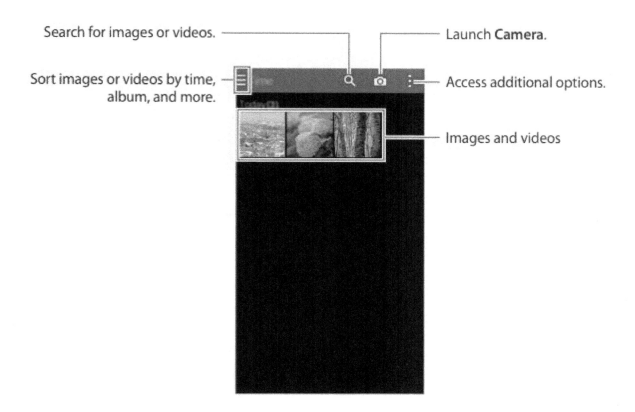

Search for images or videos. ——— Launch **Camera**.

Sort images or videos by time, album, and more. ——— Access additional options.

——— Images and videos

Send the image to others. ———————————— Modify the image.

Move to the previous screen. —— ———— Access additional options.

Search for other devices to view ———— Delete the image.
the image.

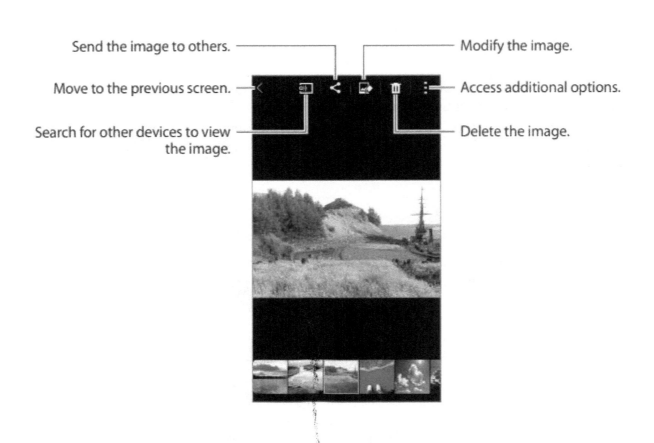

Internet

Browsing Websites

For browsing various websites, you have to tap on the "Internet" option from your Apps screen. After this, you can tap in the address field and enter the address you wish to visit.

Bookmark the current webpage. —   — Open the webpage window manager.

Read an article using **Reader**. —   — Access additional options.

— Refresh the current webpage.

Move to the home page. —   — View saved pages.

Move to the previously-visited page. —   — View bookmarked webpages.

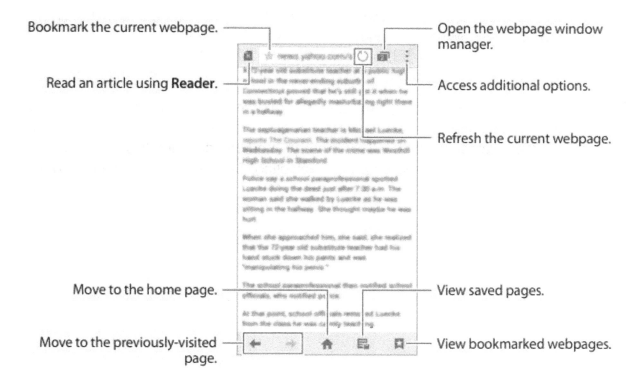

Manage Frequently Visited Webpages

You can make your life a whole lot easier by marking your frequently visited pages as your favorites so than you can access them as quickly as possible later on. To do this, go onto the "Internet" from your Apps Screen. From there, tap onto the home icon to see you quick access list. After that, you can add in your respective website to the list by tapping onto more options and then going to "Add to Quick Access".

If you want to delete a certain webpage from this list, then you can do so by holding onto the icon and then dragging in towards the "Delete" option.

Manage Website History

For managing your website history, tap onto the "Internet" from your Apps Screen. For there, go onto you bookmarks icon and tap into "History". You can clear your history by going onto more options and then "Clear History". You can also delete your webpages in your history by tapping into more options, selecting "Delete", and then tapping onto "Done".

S Health

About the feature

This app helps you to keep track of the amount of calories you consume and the amount of calories you end up burning by taking in your respective information and statistics. The app also helps to by telling you what it thinks your exercise and diet plan should be like so that you can be healthy and fit for the rest of your life. You can access "S Health" by taping onto it from your Apps Screen.

Features of the App

The Exercise feature in the S Health App manages and sets the goals of your exercise for you. Through this feature, you can check and record the various exercise related information such as speed, quantities, and calories burnt. When you have involved yourself in some outdoor exercise, you can use this feature to listen to some music, take lots of photos, and also check the location you are at.

The Pedometer feature in the app helps count the overall amount of steps you have taken.

The Food feature in the app helps to keep track of the amount of calories you consume.

S Health Startup

When you are just starting out with this app, you are required to first read and agree with all the terms and conditions of the app. Once that is done, you can set up your personal profile on it.

Voice Features

S Voice

This special app lets you make use of your voice to command your phone into performing a particular feature. You can access this app by going onto your Apps Screen or by pressing your home button two times. You can easily deactivate the home button access of this app by going onto settings, and then from there deselecting the option of "Open via the Home Key".

Language Setting

You can set the language for this app by going onto further options, then tapping on settings, and then finally selecting "Language".

S Voice Usage

Upon launching of the app, voice recognition will begin and the icon for the microphone will turn to red. After this, your device is ready for your voice command. When your phone acknowledges your command, the icon of the microphone will turn from red to green and the devise will then perform what you told it to do.

For the voce feature to work properly, you will have to ensure that there is not much background noise, you are speaking into your device clearly, you use only your original accent to speak, and you do not make use of any slang or offensive words and terminologies.

Voice Recorder

Voice Memos Recoding

From your Apps Screen, go onto "Voice Recorder". Tap onto the recoding icon to start the process of recording. Once that has begun, you can speak into your phone's microphone which is located at the bottom of your phone. Press the pause' icon whenever you wish to take a little break. For canceling a recording, simply press the cross icon. When you have finished recording a particular thing, you can press on the stop icon.

You have the option of limiting background noise while recording by simply going on "Settings", and then selecting the option of "Noise Reduction".

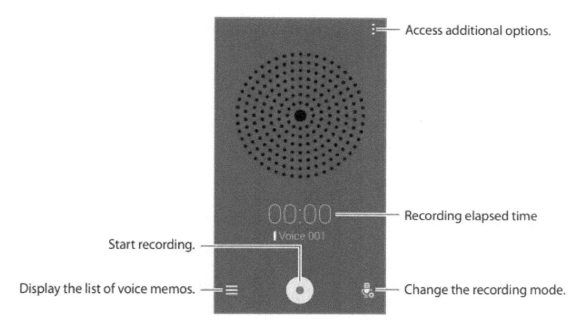

Voice Search

You can make use of this app in order to search for various webpages with your voice. Initiate this app by going onto your Apps screen and then tapping onto "Voice Search". After this, you can speak of any keyword that you would like your device to search for after the option of "Speak Now" comes onto your screen.

Car Mode

You can make use of this mode in order to control your phone while you drive without interference or hesitation. With this feature, you will be free to listen to music or your incoming messages without even having to touch your phone. All this can be done by commanding your phone through the use f your voice. In order to activate this feature, you can go onto your quick setting panel and then tap onto "Car Mode".

Multimedia

Music

You can access your "Music" app by going onto your Apps screen. After this, you can choose a category of music and then a song your want to listen to. Once that is done, you can tap on play.

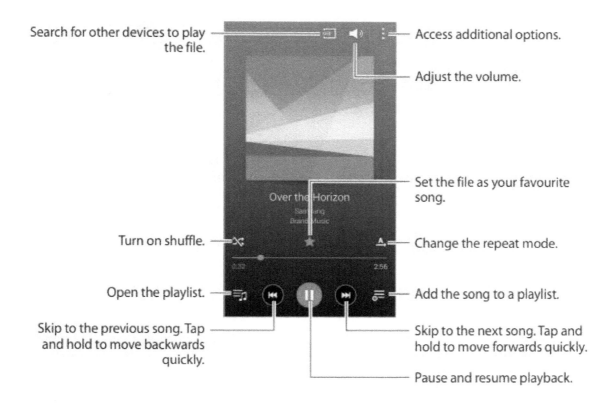

Search for other devices to play the file.

Access additional options.

Adjust the volume.

Set the file as your favourite song.

Turn on shuffle.

Change the repeat mode.

Open the playlist.

Add the song to a playlist.

Skip to the previous song. Tap and hold to move backwards quickly.

Skip to the next song. Tap and hold to move forwards quickly.

Pause and resume playback.

Playlist Creation

You can create your own playlist(s) by simply going onto "Music" from your Apps screen, then tapping onto the "Playlists" option. From here, you can go to "Create Playlist". In this option, you will have the opportunity to create your own playlist title, and then tapping on the "+" sign to include all the songs that you would like to have in that respective playlist. You can then finally select "Done" once you are through with everything.

Video

You can play any particular video that you have by simply going onto your Apps screen and then tapping on "Video" from there.

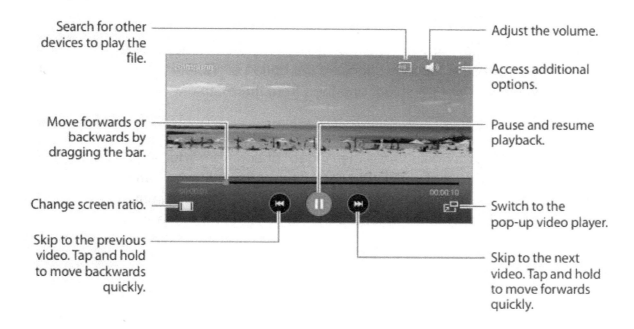

Search for other devices to play the file.

Adjust the volume.

Access additional options.

Move forwards or backwards by dragging the bar.

Pause and resume playback.

Change screen ratio.

Switch to the pop-up video player.

Skip to the previous video. Tap and hold to move backwards quickly.

Skip to the next video. Tap and hold to move forwards quickly.

Share and Delete Your Videos

To share a video, you can simply go on "Video" from your Apps screen. From there go on other options and choose "Select". From there, select any video that you would like to share, and then in other options choose "Share Via". After this, you can choose a sharing avenue that you desire.

You can delete any video you wish easily by going onto the "Video" option in your Apps Screen, and then from other options choosing the option of "Delete". You, then, select the respective video you want deleted, and then from there tap on "Done".

Video Editing

You can edit your videos by going onto the "Video" option from your Apps screen, and then first selecting a video that you would like edited. After that, you can tap on more option, then tap on Edit, and then select the option stating "Video Trimmer". After you are done with the editing, you can select "Done", and then enter a particular name for that file, after which you can tap on OK. Your video will then be officially saved. You also have the option of getting your videos edited using "Video Editor".

Security

Fingerprint Scanner

Registration

You can register your fingerprints by going onto your Apps screen and then tapping onto settings. From there you go on to the "Finger Scanner" option and then tap on the option of "Fingerprint Manager". You also have the option of getting more that one fingerprint registered on the device. All you have to do is tap on the "+" option once you are done with one fingerprint.

The process of registering is simple. Put your finger over the fingerprint region which is located below the screen. Now drag the finger down till it reaches the "Home" button. Repeat the process until the phone recognizes your print and registers it in the device. Once registered, you can unlock your phone using your fingerprint. Take care not to use the tip of your ginger or bend your finger in any way while registering.

The device might also ask for an alternate password for the verification process in case you want to use that process for unlocking your phone instead of the fingerprint process.

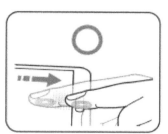 

Fingerprint Management

You have the option of renaming or even deleting your already existing fingerprints. All you have to do for that is go on to your Apps screen, and then tap onto settings. From there, go on to the "Finger Printer" and tap on "Fingerprint Manager".

You can delete your registered fingerprints by selecting "Deregister" following by selecting the fingerprint you want deleted. Then simply tap onto the 'trash' symbol and click on OK.

You can rename your fingerprints by going on "Select" then selecting your required fingerprint, following by tapping on the "Edit" option marked by a 'pencil', and then entering a different name for your fingerprint. Click on OK to save your changes.

Alternate Password Change

You always have the option of changing your alternate password that you might like to use instead of fingerprint scanning. All you have to do is go onto your Apps screen. From there, tap on "settings", then "Fingerprint Scanner", and then "Change Alternative Password". After that, you will be required to insert your current password and then your new password, and then click on OK. Your new password will officially be set then.

Fingerprint Unlocking

You can use your officially registered fingerprints to scan and then unlock your phone screen. This can be done by going on your Apps screen and then going on "Settings". From there, click on "Finger Scanner", then "Screen Lock", then Fingerprint. You can also set this by going on "Lock Screen" from your "Settings", then going on "Screen Lock", and then "Fingerprint".

Verifying Your Samsung Account Password with your Fingerprints

You can make use of your fingerprints for verifying the password for your Samsung account instead of having to enter a respective password for it. For instance, this can be done when purchasing your App content.

For doing this, you will have to go onto your Apps screen. From there go on "Settings", and then tap on "Finger Scanner". From there, go on to "Verify Samsung Account" and turn the "verify Samsung Account" tab towards the right hand side. After this, you will be required to enter your password and click on "Confirm".

Private Mode

Private mode in the phone helps users to hide certain content within your phone so that other unauthorized people are unable to access that content. This content could be anything from certain documents to even images.

Method

In order to hide certain important things on your phone, you can go onto your Apps screen. Over here, go on "Settings" and then click on "Private Mode". Here, you will be required to swipe the switch of "Private Mode" towards the right hand side. You can also do this by another method of going to quick setting panel, and then form there going onto "Private Mode", after which you can switch it on. If you have never set this up before, then be sure to put some unlock code along with a PIN for backup.

After this, you can choose your items that you would want to hide by holding those items and ticking them in order to select them. You can then choose "Move to Private" or "Move", then "Private", and then finally "Move Here".

Private Content Viewing

The hidden contents in private mode can only be seen when that mode has been activated. Once active, you can go on your Apps screen, tap onto "My Files", and then go to "Private". From there you can view all you hidden items. You will also be needing an unlock code which you preciously set up specifically for Private Mode.

Safety

Emergency Mode

The emergency mode in your S5 is used in certain emergency cases where your phone battery is running low and you wish to conserve it. When this mode is switched on, your battery consumption will reduce significantly by turning off or reducing a few of the phone features. For instance, you screen brightness will decrease and your Wi-Fi or mobile data will switch off. This feature also lets you use features like sound alarms, flash, along with sending location details to your friends and family so they may find you in time.

Activation

To activate the emergency mode, you will be required to hold onto the power button. After this a few options will appear. Tap into "Emergency Mode". You can also go to "Emergency Mode" by visiting your Apps screen. From there go onto "Settings", after which you can go to "Safety Assistance", and then finally "Emergency Mode".

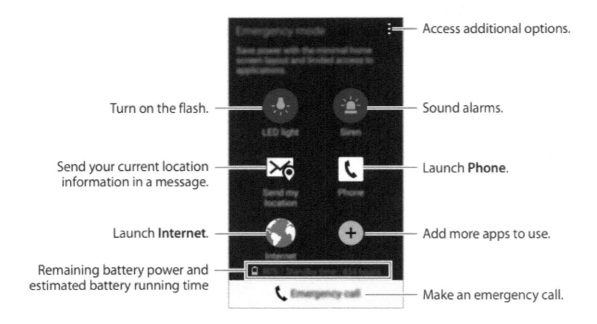

Access additional options.

Turn on the flash. — Sound alarms.

Send your current location information in a message. — Launch **Phone**.

Launch **Internet**. — Add more apps to use.

Remaining battery power and estimated battery running time — Make an emergency call.

Deactivation

For deactivation of the emergency mode, you can hold your phone's power button and then tap onto the "Emergency Mode" button. You can also go to "Disable Emergency Mode" through more options.

Help Messages

These help messages (in the case of an emergency) can be sent to a list of contacts you have already decided upon. It works by pressing quickly on your Power Button thrice in order to send messages or make calls to your selected contacts.

Selecting Contacts

You can select your emergency contacts by going onto your Apps screen and from there tapping on "Settings". In the settings option, you will find "Safety Assistance". Tap on this option and then go on "Manage Primary Contacts". In this, you can go on "Create Primary Contact". Tap onto "Create New Contact" in this option, and enter your relevant information. You can also tap onto "Select from Contacts to add a contact that already exists in your phone.

Help Message Setting

To set you help messages, go onto you Apps screen and then tap onto the "Settings" option. From there go onto "Safety Assistance", and then "Send Help Messages". Activate that option and then choose the content that you would like to send out to your contacts.

Help Message Sending

When you are faced with an emergency, you can press your Power Button thrice in a quick manner. This will automatically send your composed help message to your emergency contact list along with the information pertaining to your location.

Geo News – (Notification for Severe Weather)

You can make use of this feature for receiving notifications pertaining to the conditions of severe weather of the location you are at. The feature is great at identifying your present location and gives you all the information the app has available regarding any disasters that are bound to happen within your vicinity.

Setting Up Notifications for Severe Weather

In order to set up these notifications, you can go onto your Apps Screen and then tap onto settings. From your settings option, you will have access to the option of "Safety Assistance". Go onto that, then tap onto "Geo News", and then activate it.

Receive Notifications

You can receive your notifications by going onto your Apps screen and then tapping onto "Settings". From here, you can go onto "Safety Assistance" and then activate "Geo News".

Warning Notifications

Tick the option of Notification pop-ups. By doing this, you will get a notification on your device in case the weather conditions become worse than what they are at present. You can even send emergency messages and make your emergency calls to a bunch of contact you have preset for exactly such an emergency situation. You will be able to do all of this by going onto your pop up window.

Watch Notifications

In the case of weather conditions that are not that severe, you will get the notifications on your status bar which is positioned right on top of your phone screen. This information will be provided on your widget for "Geo New".

Making use of your Widget for Geo News

You can make use of your widget for Geo News to information about the various disasters pertaining to your area. To go onto this widget, you have to go to your Home screen, and then from there scroll towards the left hand side and tap onto the widget you will find for "Geo News".

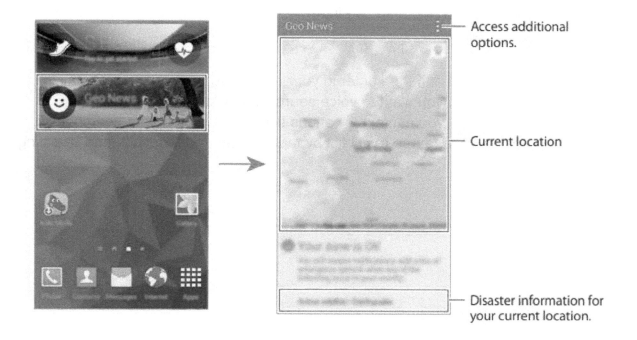

Access additional options.

Current location

Disaster information for your current location.

Utilities

S Finder

This finder app will help you to search for different content with the help of the internet on your particular phone. You have the option of applying different filters and looking at your history of searches. To access your S finder app, you will have to go to your notifications panel and then tap onto "S Finder".

Content Search

Tap onto your search field and then enter in your respective keyword or even say in your respective keyword if you want to voice search it. In order to achieve more refinement in your results, you can apply various filters underneath your search field. You can even update your search result list by tapping onto more options and selecting "Refresh".

Search History Management

You can delete your search history by tapping onto more options, and the going onto "Settings". In settings, you will find the option of "Delete History. Select that.

You can even set your phone in a way that I never has search results saved. In order to do this, you will have to tap onto more options, and then from there going onto "Settings". Once on settings, you will be required to deselect the option of "Save Search History".

S Planner

You can make use of this app to manage your various everyday tasks and events. Access this app by tapping onto the option of S Planner which will be located on your Apps Screen.

Change view mode. —  — Access additional options.

Go to today's date. — Create events or tasks.

On this app, you can go onto more options to make use of the options of "Search", "Go to", "Sync", "Delete", "Settings", and "Calendars".

Task or Event Creation

For creation of tasks and events, you can access your S Planner from your Apps screen. After this, you can tap onto the + sign and then add in a particular date for your tasks or events. Once this is done, you will be required to fill in details of the task or event at hand. You can tap on "Save" once all the details have been filled out.

Syncing of Tasks and Events with your respective Accounts

In order to sync these tasks and events with your respective accounts, you will have to first access your S Planner via your Apps Screen. After this, you can go onto more options and then select "Sync". In order to add in your accounts, you will have to tap onto more options, and then go on "Calendars". From here, you will be required to tap onto "Add Accounts". After this, you will simply have to choose your respective account, and then sign yourself in.

If you want to change your account's syncing, then you can simply go back to "Settings, and then from there go onto "Accounts".

Deleting Tasks or Events

In order to carry out the deleting process, you will first be required to go onto your Apps Screen and then tap onto "S Planner". From here, you can delete your respective tasks or events by going onto more options and then tapping onto "Delete". Once you are through with this, you can tap "Done", and that's pretty much all there is to it. If you want to delete a certain task or event while you view it, you can simply tap onto the trash can icon and then select OK.

Sharing Tasks or Events

In order to share your tasks and events, you will first have to access your S Planner through your Apps screen. A much touted feature of the Samsung lineup, the S Planner is widely regarded as a lifesaver by many. Once you have accessed the app, you can go onto more options and then choose "Share Via". Proceed to choose whatever method you want to share with.

Kids Mode

This widget is a great way for your kids to have fun and have a safe environment to interact in at the same time. This is because, Kids Mode helps to put a restriction or limit on certain content and apps. To access this app, you will have to first download it and install your respective app widget. When you have successfully installed your widget, you will be required to go onto your Home Screen, tap onto Kids Mode, and then select "Install". A successfully installed widget will make an appearance on your Apps and home screens. In order to tart this app, you will have to rap onto Kids Mode, either via your Apps screen or your Home screen.

This is how the Home Screen of Kids Mode looks like:

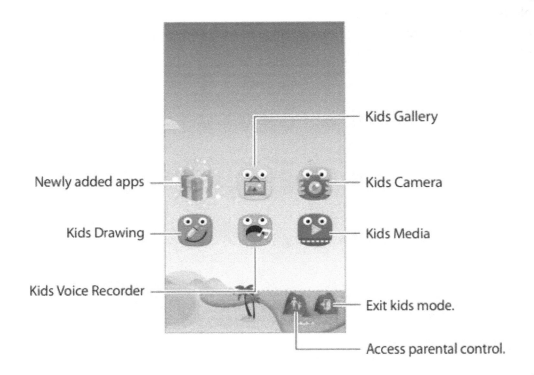

Play Area in Kids Mode

You can open up the play area for your Kids Mode by scrolling towards the right hand side of your Home Screen. The best part is, your kids will be able to interact with all the background objects and characters on your screen this way.

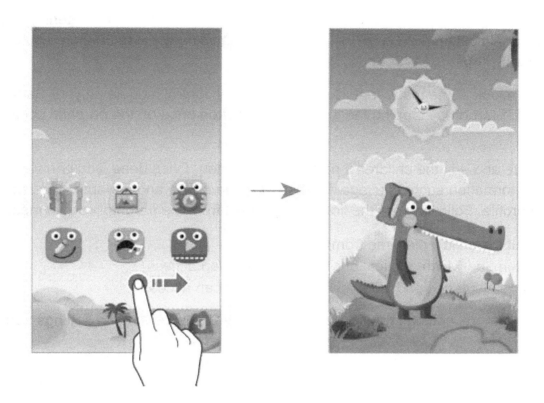

Parental Control

You can make use of this feature in order to set a certain amount of restrictions for your children so that certain apps and content remains out of their reach. This can be done through the use of usage time limits, kid's mode settings, and a lot more.

The parental control can be activated by tapping the home screen and entering your personal identification number (PIN). To exit, one can simply press the home screen button again.

Let's take a look at the many features of the parental control module on your Samsung Galaxy S5. Start off by tapping the more options button once on the parental control screen.

First, create and edit the children's profile to get started. Once done, you can view relevant information such as usage duration from the profile and the apps frequented from the profile. Following are the limits you can set from the parental control module:

- Limit the child's playtime from the profile
- Determine which applications should be allowed access
- Pinpoint images and videos which the profile can access

To access general settings for the profile, you can visit the kid's mode settings panel.

Magnifier

In the ease-of-access tools department, the Samsung Galaxy S5 brings you the magnifier tool. To access the tool at convenience, one can add it the phone's home screen. To do so, identify an empty area on the home screen, tap, and then hold for a few seconds. In the screen that pops open, select widgets, and hold the magnifier widget from the menu. Now simply drag the Magnifier widget onto the home screen, and place it wherever you deem convenient.

To use it, use the + or − buttons to manage the amount of magnification as per your preference. If need be, one can even adjust the focus of identification by manually tapping the area of focus.

Maps

The maps option is a crucial aspect in most mobile devices, more so for smartphones. The Galaxy S5's map app can be used to pinpoint specific locations, get directions to wherever you want to go, and even pinpoint the location of the device itself in case it is stolen, lost, or misplaced. To use it, tap the Maps app from the application drawer. Keep in mind though; the Maps app on the S5 may not be available for some regions, depending on the local phone service provider.

Locations

By far the most commonly used functionality of the Maps app is to search for locations. This can be done by typing in either the address or just a keyword on the app. Available information on the location be accessed by selecting it once it is found.

Getting Directions

Once you search a location, you can also get step-by-step directions for it, complete with start and end points. Tap the relevant button, select your preferred mode of travel, and you're good to go!

Tips to saving your Samsung S5's Battery Life

Most smartphone users often complain about their battery life and how it runs out a bit too quickly. There is no doubt that people are constantly using their phones and therefore, even the battery you have available with you does not seem sufficient at all. A few of the people will even try to utilize the last bit of battery that is left in their Samsung S5.

For the purpose of your battery, there are a few tips that you can use to save it and make the best possible use of your Samsung Galaxy S5 battery. Go to the next page to find out about these tips.

Brightness of Your Display

The brightness levels of your Samsung Galaxy S5 display greatly affect the battery life of your phone. Therefore, you should lower your brightness considerably or auto adjust it so that your phone can handle the brightness levels for you. The option of 'auto adjust screen tone' will also help to save your battery life considerably according to Samsung. This is done by brightness adjustment according to whatever your display is showing at that moment.

Display Timeout

Your display timeout is a feature in your phone that will let your phone turn off after the set time has run out. In your Samsung S5, you can set this time to as low as 15 seconds, after which your display will be turned off if your phone is not in use. This helps to save battery immensely and will not even annoy or bother you by staying on.

Power Saving Mode in the Samsung Galaxy S5

The power saving mode option in your Galaxy S5 will also be immensely helpful in saving battery. This will give you two options. The first one is the normal power saving mode in which you have the option of restricting your background data because of which you will have to manually fresh your Facebook, Twitter, and email. You also have the option of limiting your phone's performance like, for instance, reducing the rate of your screen frame, processor of your phone, and completely switching off your phone's G{OS along with backlit keys. You can either activate power saving mode through an automatic phone process or choose to do it manually, whatever is more convenient to you.

The other option that you have is the ultra power saving mode, in this mode, everything will turn to grayscale, There is also a power saving mode which is much simpler in which your smartphone will become dumb because you have the limitation of only a few applications. The Wi-Fi and Bluetooth will completely get disconnected in this unless you manually change these settings later.

Wearable for Notification Use

There are three wearables that are immediately available for the Samsung Galaxy S5, and these wearables help to save your battery immensely. They do this by letting you know what notifications you receive without you having to turn on your phone display. And as we know from beforehand, your phone's display utilizes a lot of your battery power.

Good Wi-Fi as opposed to a Bad Network

If you have good Wi-Fi available for you to use, then you should make the most of it instead of relying on a bad network for your internet. Sure, many of the people do not have Wi-Fi available to them all the time, but in instances that you do have it available, you should make the most of it. A bad connection is horrible for you battery, as it will simply drain quickly and will leave your phone miserable and even hot. A phone connection will also prove to be bad for your money.

A Brief Roundup

You should now have all the information that you need regarding your Samsung Galaxy S5. The guide was designed to make your life much easier with aspect to your new phone, and the purpose of this amazing smartphone is to make your life easier in general.

With so many amazing apps and features, there is no doubt that you will have a truly wholesome experience with this phone, and you will likely start enjoying your social life a whole lot more. The phone is also great with respect to the amount of security it provides its users.